Children of the World

France

For a free color catalog describing Gareth Stevens' list of high-quality children's books, call 1-800-341-3569 (USA) or 1-800-461-9120 (Canada).

For their help in the preparation of *Children of the World: France*, the editors gratefully thank the Chancery of France, Washington, DC; United States Department of State, Bureau of Public Affairs, Office of Public Communication, Washington, DC, for unencumbered use of material in the public domain; Employment and Immigration Canada, Ottawa, Ont.; the US Immigration and Naturalization Service, Press Office, Washington, DC; and special thanks to Professor Michelle Szkilnik, Department of Romance Languages, The University of Wisconsin, Madison, Wisconsin.

Library of Congress Cataloging-in-Publication Data

France.

    (Children of the world)
    Summary: Presents the life of a twelve-year-old girl and her family living in a village in Normandy describing her home and school, daily activities, amusements, and some of the customs and celebrations of her country.
    1. France—Juvenile literature. 2. Children—France—Juvenile literature. [1. Family life—France. 2. France—Social life and customs] I. Tolan, Sally. II. Sherwood, Rhoda. III. Pierre, Philippe, ill. IV. Series.
DC17.F655   1989   944   88-42889
ISBN 1-55532-212-3

North American edition first published in 1990 by

Gareth Stevens Children's Books
RiverCenter Building, Suite 201
1555 North RiverCenter Drive
Milwaukee, Wisconsin 53212, USA

This work was originally published in shortened form consisting of section I only. Photographs copyright © 1989 by Philippe Pierre. Original text copyright © 1989 by Monique Maeno. First and originally published by Kaisei-sha Publishing Co., Ltd., Tokyo. World English rights arranged with Kaisei-sha Publishing Co., Ltd. through Japan Foreign-Rights Centre.

This format copyright © 1990 by Gareth Stevens, Inc. Additional material and maps copyright © 1990 by Gareth Stevens, Inc.

Series editor: Rhoda Irene Sherwood
Research editor: Scott Enk
Map design: Sheri Gibbs

Printed in the United States of America

1 2 3 4 5 6 7 8 9 96 95 94 93 92 91 90

Children of the World
France

Photography by
Philippe Pierre

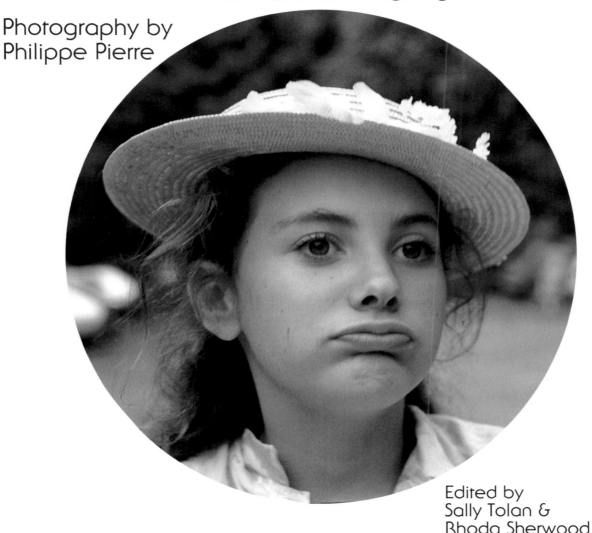

Edited by
Sally Tolan &
Rhoda Sherwood

Gareth Stevens Children's Books
MILWAUKEE

10-21-92

. . . a note about *Children of the World*:

The children of the world live in fishing towns, Arctic regions, and urban centers, on
islands and in mountain valleys, on sheep ranches and fruit farms. This series follows
one child in each country through the pattern of his or her life. Candid photographs
show the children with their families, at school, at play, and in their communities.
The text describes the dreams of the children and, often through their own words,
tells how they see themselves and their lives.

Each book also explores events that are unique to the country in which the child lives,
including festivals, religious ceremonies, and national holidays. The *Children
of the World* series does more than tell about foreign countries. It introduces the
children of each country and shows readers what it is like to be a child in that country.

. . . and about *France*:

Karine Reysset, 11 years old, lives in Belbeuf, a town near Rouen, in Normandy.
France is a country with centuries-old ties to North America. Its philosophers, explorers,
and artists, among others, have been critical in the shaping of Western history.

To enhance this book's value in libraries and classrooms, comprehensive reference
sections include current information about France's geography, demographics,
language, education, culture, industry, and natural resources. *France* also features
a bibliography, research topics, activity projects, and discussions of such subjects as
Paris, the country's history, its art, political system, and religious composition.

The living conditions and experiences of children in France have been enriched by the
concern the French people feel for their architectural wonders, their history, and their
culture. The reference sections help bring these features to life for young readers,
exploring the richness of the culture and heritage of France.

CONTENTS

The city of Rouen along the banks of the Seine, the best-known river in France.

LIVING IN FRANCE:
Karine, a Girl of Normandy

Eleven-year-old Karine Reysset lives in Belbeuf, a town near the city of Rouen, in Normandy, in northwest France. Karine is a good-natured girl. When she smiles, her brown eyes sparkle. But her face can change quickly from a nose-wrinkling grin to a serious expression. The name *Karine* means "pure."

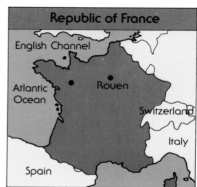

Their brick and stucco house.

The sunny backyard.

Top to bottom: Pascal, Claudine, Karine, Tanguy, baby Pauline.

Karine's father, Pascal, is an urban planner who decides about land use, plans buildings, and improves the appearance of urban areas. Her mother, Claudine, teaches primary school and serves on the Belbeuf town council. Karine's brother, Tanguy, is eight and in the third grade. Her baby sister, Pauline, is fourteen months old.

Although busy with their jobs, Pascal and Claudine spend time with the children. The Reyssets walk in nearby fields and woods or sing or just talk. Sometimes they play at dressing up or cook together. Even baby Pauline joins in the fun. When relatives visit, everyone gets pretty silly.

In April, the apple trees are covered with white blossoms.

They set out their picnic lunch on a quilt:
fruit, bread, cheese, sausage, and ham.

A Picnic

A great day for a picnic! The family fills baskets and sets off in the car. The road is called the "Fruit Route," for it follows the Seine River and curves among orchards. People buy the ripe fruit to enjoy as they travel or picnic. The pink-tinged white blossoms will soon fall, so the family hurries in order to see them at their loveliest.

Opposite: This spring the trees have bloomed late because the weather has been cool and rainy.

Karine and Claudine sit on the lawn in front of a great French country house, or château.

Normandy

Normandy got its name from the Norsemen who conquered the area in AD 911. It is a land of rolling green hills, granite cliffs, and vast Atlantic beaches. The French love it for its historic buildings, its orchards, the heavy rains, and the brown and white dairy cattle.

In the countryside are *châteaus* — large, elegant country houses — and even castles. These once belonged to French nobility. Now, while some belong to descendants of the original owners, others belong to organizations that buy them because they are too big and expensive to maintain as private homes. Many charge visitors, who want to see the beautiful rooms and elegant furnishings and to stroll around the grounds. Karine and Claudine sometimes visit the château at Belbeuf.

Many venerable churches and cathedrals remain in France, where most of the people have been Roman Catholic since the country's early days. In Rouen is the Cathédrale de Notre Dame, made famous in paintings by Claude Monet. The church that Claudine and Karine attend is old, with exquisitely carved statues and stained-glass windows.

Rouen is the chief river port of France. Because it is at the center of rich farming country, it is a center for food processing and for trade in cattle, grain, and wine. It is the capital of its section of Normandy, and like any other good-sized city, it has stores and offices, many old and beautiful churches, and public and governmental buildings.

In Rouen is the Tour de Jeanne D'Arc (Tower of Joan of Arc), built to remind people of the girl from Rouen who led French troops against the British in a battle at Orléans. French soldiers on the side of the British later captured her.

A church court had Joan of Arc put to death in 1431 because it decided she had committed heresy. Joan, a Roman Catholic, committed heresy when she made statements that went against the official beliefs of the Roman Catholic Church. Her heresy was that she claimed she had heard the voices of saints telling her to go to war. The Roman Catholic Church declared her a saint in 1920.

Karine reads her prayer book in church.

Karine, beside her church.

Karine admires a traditional Normandy farmhouse.

The Tour de Jeanne D'Arc is not the only reminder of strife that has occurred in Rouen. During the German occupation of France during World War II, Rouen suffered severe damage from bombing by the Allies, who were trying to drive the Germans out of France. While some signs of damage remain, most of the damage has been repaired over the years.

Today Rouen is considered a bustling beauty of a city. Located in the center of this fertile land, it provides jobs for many people in Karine's small town, Belbeuf, and for other small towns in the outlying areas.

Today many people of Normandy live in modern houses like the Reyssets', but the traditional houses of the countryside and towns are half-timbered. The walls are reinforced by a wooden framework. This framework, which gives the Norman house its distinctive look, is filled in with plaster and sometimes brick. The roofs of these houses are steep and shingled.

Farmers who lived in these half-timbered houses used to wear wooden shoes that would keep their feet dry as they walked in muddy fields or farmyards, doing their chores. Today farmers are more likely to wear rubber boots when the ground is wet.

A hand-carved wooden shoe from the museum shop.

The sleepy Reyssets breakfast together.

The children try to pose with a doll . . .

. . . but soon start giggling.

A Spring Morning

A bright spring morning! Everything sparkles in the sunlight. Karine and Tanguy, bringing Pauline with them, run into their parents' room, calling, "Get up, we're hungry!"

Karine washes her face and then gets breakfast ready. On the table she sets bread, jam, butter, cereal, coffee, and cocoa. Many French people have just *café au lait*, coffee with hot milk, for breakfast.

Admiring the baby and teasing Dad.

Claudine prepares boiled eggs and ham and sets out some cereal for those who prefer it. Pascal comes to the table, still half asleep. Tanguy sits down in high spirits, chattering away to the family.

It is the weekend, so after breakfast everyone dresses and goes out to enjoy the yard. Tanguy invites a friend over to play, and they all relax in the sun.

The living room.

Pascal and Claudine's bedroom.

15

Karine Helps Out

In France, every town has its *supermarché*, or supermarket, but France is also famous for its small food shops.

Bread is sold in *boulangeries*, or bakeries, and tarts and other pastries are sold in *patisseries*, or pastry shops. Because she knows she can rely on Karine, Claudine often sends her to the boulangerie for crusty loaves of bread, called *baguettes*, or to the supermarché for milk.

Karine likes to ramble through the streets, looking in windows at toys, clothes, and books. Sometimes she finds herself daydreaming and realizes she'd better move more quickly. When she gets to the boulangerie, she chooses a small roll for herself to munch on while she walks home with the family's bread.

Bread in many shapes and sizes.

16

Karine also does her share of chores around the house. While Claudine tucks Pauline into bed at night, Karine often straightens up the kitchen. After loading the dishwasher, she sweeps the floor and pushes all the chairs back in under the table. Karine likes their modern home with its automatic dishwasher. She's still a little too short to reach the sink comfortably when she has to wash any dishes.

Karine also baby-sits for baby Pauline and Tanguy when Claudine and Pascal go out. The task she especially likes is feeding Chaton, the family cat.

Sometimes Karine complains. She thinks Tanguy should help more. But then she realizes that he is too small to do much yet. Still, she is looking forward to his getting bigger.

Shaking crumbs from the tablecloth.

It's time for Chaton to have supper.

Karine sweeps up the dust and crumbs . . .

After doing her chores, Karine likes to retreat to a place where she can daydream, study, or putter about.

Her bedroom is her quiet spot. Here she has a collection of miniatures, a few dolls she still occasionally plays with, other toys, and her books. Sometimes she likes to rearrange her belongings. Sometimes she prefers to sit at her desk and do schoolwork. Other times she just wants to flop down on her comfortable bed and read a good book.

Karine also likes to read in her room before going to sleep, but she does not stay up late. Like most French children, she turns off the light by 9:00 p.m.

. . . and loads dishes into the dishwasher . . .

. . . and tidies up her room.

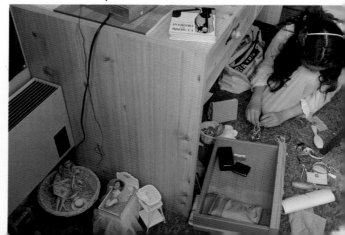

Her reward is a quiet time to read.

Her treasures rest on shelves.

And more sit on her desktop, in front of the map.

It's hard to decide when there are so many choices.

Karine's parents wait patiently and entertain Pauline.

Starting Junior High

The whole week before Karine is to start junior high school is a busy one. She goes shopping in Rouen for schoolbooks, pens, notebooks, and other school supplies. She also needs new clothes: a sweater, a skirt, pants, and a few tops.

On school days Karine gets up at seven o'clock. She hurries Tanguy along in the bathroom and eats a quick breakfast. She takes a few minutes to decide what she wants to wear to school. At quarter to eight she runs out to catch the bus. A little later, Tanguy goes off to his school, and Pascal and Claudine leave for work, dropping Pauline off at the day-care center on the way.

Karine urges Tanguy to hurry. She downs a quick breakfast before school. The last one out locks the door.

It takes about twenty minutes for Karine's bus to get from her house to school. Because there is no junior high school in Belbeuf, Karine goes to one in nearby Bonsecours. In France a junior high school is called a *collège*, and a senior high school is called a *lycée*. After four years of collège, some students go on for three years in a lycée to prepare for the *baccalauréat* exams that they must pass to enter a university. Other students attend technical schools to prepare for work in the skilled trades, such as carpentry, electronics, and mechanics.

The time goes quickly because Karine talks and laughs with a friend.

Karine's school. In France, a junior high school is called a collège.

The students chatter before classes begin.

The first term starts in September and ends at Christmas. The second term runs until Easter, and the third ends in June. Students get report cards at the end of every term. Grades are based on averages of all grades given on homework and tests. Students who do not receive passing grades must repeat the year. Karine studies hard and doesn't worry about failing any classes.

In French class, Madame Dufour talks about the lives of children in Africa.

Karine's School

School begins at 8:30. Karine has six classes on Mondays, Tuesdays, and Fridays, and is in school until 4:00. On Thursdays she has seven classes and is in school until 5:00. She is also at school until 10:30 a.m. on Saturdays, but has no school on Wednesdays or Sundays.

She is studying music, French, English, mathematics, history, geography, biology, physics, drawing, crafts, and physical education. Her favorite subjects are French, English, and drawing. Mathematics is her weakest subject, but it is required for entrance to the university, so she works hard at it.

Lots of books for just a small book bag.

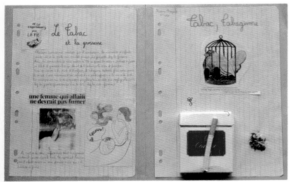

A report on the damage to health from smoking.

In French class, the students study grammar and spelling in their textbook. They also read and discuss other assigned books, write essays, and memorize poetry and parts of plays.

In 1635, the French founded a group called the *Académie Française*. The purpose of the group is to honor scholars, writers, and other people who work to better the world. But another of its jobs is to observe how the French language is used and how it develops. The 40 people chosen to be in the academy are careful about letting foreign words slip into the French vocabulary, and they don't like slang — whether foreign or French!

Karine likes to lead discussions and to read aloud for her class.

Some students go home to eat lunch, but Karine eats in the school cafeteria. The menu changes every day, but she complains that no matter what is served, it all tastes the same. Teachers supervise the lunch hour. Students and teachers are hungry after their long morning of classes, so everyone finishes eating within half an hour.

Karine sees her friends at lunchtime and after school.

On nice days, students go into the schoolyard after lunch and play ball games or hopscotch or jump rope. Clusters of boys and girls chat. The boys talk mostly about bicycle racing, soccer, tennis — and girls. The girls are more likely to talk about friends, fashions, families — and boys. In bad weather, students stay in their classrooms and read or talk. The teachers are always nearby keeping an eye on everything. Children who get in trouble on the playground or in class may have to stay after school or do special assignments.

Karine and her classmates smile for the camera. She's in the center, in the blue coat.

About seven hundred students attend the four grades of Karine's school. Her grade level is divided into eight sections, or classes, each named for a color. Karine is in the Pink Class. There are twenty-eight students in the Pink Class. The homeroom teacher is Madame Dufour, who also teaches Karine's French class. In French junior high schools, students have a different teacher for each subject and have foreign language classes for the first time. In most schools, students can choose one of several languages. Karine chose English.

The school day ends at 4:00 p.m., and Karine rides the bus straight home. Claudine finishes work about 4:00 and picks Pauline up at the day-care center. After school, Karine and Tanguy have a snack of bread and jam with fruit juice or milk or, if the weather is cold, hot cocoa. Then they settle down to do their homework. Soon Pascal comes home from work, and around 7:00 the whole family sits down together for dinner. Some of Karine's favorite foods for dinner are fried potatoes, chicken, and fish.

27

Sharing a shady bench before the Arc de Triomphe.

Off to Paris

One Wednesday afternoon, Karine, her mother, and her best friend Alexandra set off for Paris. It takes the three travelers about an hour and a half to go from Rouen to Paris by train.

Their first stop is the famous Eiffel Tower. From the top they see the great city spread before them, in all directions, with the silvery Seine River curving through its center. Then they go to see the nearby Arc de Triomphe, built in the 1800s as a monument to Napoleon's troops.

They spend an hour at the Musée Grévin, a wax museum with figures of famous poets, entertainers, and politicians. Looking at the life-sized figures of France's president, François Mitterrand, and prime minister, Michel Rocard, Karine can hardly keep from touching them. The exhibit also intrigues Alexandra, but the figures look so real that they seem a little spooky, and she is glad when it is time to leave.

The Geode in the Parc de la Villette.

A panoramic view of Paris with the Eiffel Tower in the distance.

Next, the three go to the Parc de la Villette. There, the Geode, a new, futuristic theater with a great silver sphere for a roof, has films about space and nature. The film that is being shown today is *Water and Humankind*.

On the train heading back to Rouen, Karine thinks about Paris. It is so different from home that sometimes she feels as if she is in a foreign country.

Waiting to board the train back to Rouen.

29

Karine's Baptism

Most French people consider themselves Roman Catholic, but fewer than half attend church on Sunday. Children are usually baptized when they are babies, but Karine's mother is Catholic and her father isn't, so they did not have Karine baptized when she was a baby.

Karine wears a new dress for her baptism.

The priest reads the baptism vows to Karine while the family looks on.

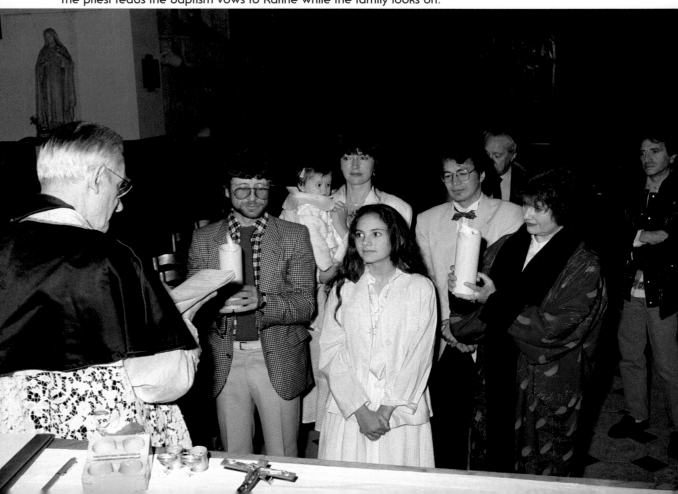

But now Karine wants to become a Catholic because she has been feeling sad and confused. When she was nine, her three-month-old brother, Laïc, died suddenly. His death shocked and hurt Karine.

Then she started going to church with her mother. The Catholic Church seemed to answer her questions. After talking it over with her mother, she decided to become a Catholic. Her father did not object.

Karine has invited her favorite relatives to the baptism. White flowers rest on the church altar, and Karine wears a pure white dress. She listens intently to the priest and vows to live as a Catholic. Afterward everyone goes to the house and shares a festive meal of roast duck, olive stew, cheese, and cake.

The honored guest, at the head of the table.

Beautifully arranged, delicious food for Karine.

Pascal carves the roast duck.

Karine and her cousins pose at the château.

A Visit with Karine's Grandparents

Pascal's parents live in Draveil, a lake town outside Paris. In the middle of the town is a large old château, rented cheaply for parties and other events. Every summer, Karine's grandparents and their neighbors party there, and Karine and her family are invited.

Testing to see if the lamb is done.

Pascal helps serve food at his parents' party.

Tables and chairs are set up in the garden. Music is playing. The food includes lamb and sausages baked for many hours in a pit outdoors. After eating, everyone dances.

Karine likes this chance to be with her relatives. Her white-haired grandfather bicycles around town, swims in the lake, talks with his grandchildren, and loves telling jokes and making people laugh. Karine's grandmother is a quiet, gentle woman who loves it when her grandchildren visit. Karine likes to talk to her.

Karine has so many cousins that some don't know each other well, so Karine, who is oldest, always takes charge whenever they are together. This is a job she likes. It's fun getting reacquainted with the older cousins, and the little ones are cute. Karine's favorite cousin is Marie. She sees her at least once a month.

Karine and Pascal whoop it up in the pool.

Down the big water slide!

Karine's family and friends soak in a hot tub.

October Pleasures

In October, the trees and hedges glow with red, brown, orange, and yellow leaves. It is so beautiful outdoors that no one wants to stay inside. On Saturdays and Sundays Karine and her family are out as much as possible.

Karine's town, Belbeuf, stands on a rise overlooking the Seine River, where the climate invites people to be out of doors. Nearby orchards provide cider and fruit as well as jobs for many people in the area. Piling into the car, the family heads for the orchards.

Romping through the autumn woods.

Leaf sprites smile toward the sky.

Reaching for the best apple.

The area around Karine's home is in what geologists call the Paris Basin. Over thousands of years, layers of sediment have built up here, and these layers have created rich soil. The Seine River, which drains the Paris Basin, has provided a way for farmers to transport their produce northwest to the English Channel and southeast to Paris.

But one sacrifice has been that in order to find land for grazing and farming, the French have had to cut down their once vast beech and oak forests. Now forests remain primarily in the mountains, although in recent years this seems to be changing somewhat.

At the end of the 19th century, the people began programs to protect forests and have reestablished trees on 25% of the land. Karine has learned about these programs in school and now wants to visit a forest.

Karine sits beside a pile of apples to be used for making cider.

People in the area also have their own gardens at home. Most houses have gardens and fields attached, where people grow vegetables and tend fruit trees. Strawberries ripen in May, and later in summer raspberry bushes glow with berries. Many families pick the berries to eat and to make jam. Most of the people living in Belbeuf, however, are not farmers but work in nearby Rouen.

Limbs of the apple trees sag with ripening fruit. Karine picks a crisp red apple and eats it right away. Orchard owners harvest their apples, some to keep and some to sell. Some apple growers pile big mounds of apples to put through their presses for cider.

Early fall is a good time to find mushrooms — and chestnuts.

Mushroom Hunting

On a damp Sunday, Karine's family goes to a nearby woods to pick mushrooms. Tanguy wears his rain boots, Karine wears her red raincoat, and Claudine and Pascal carry baskets and knives. Pauline rolls around in the fallen leaves. Karine and Tanguy flop down in the leaves with her and Pascal pulls them up. They begin to play, pushing and tumbling among the rustling leaves. The air is full of the warm smell of earth and the sharper scent of the drying leaves.

Now it is time to start hunting for mushrooms. Everyone except little Pauline picks up a knife to cut mushrooms. They pick only the mushrooms called *cèpes*. All the others they are careful not to touch, for they could be poisonous. Pascal checks all the mushrooms that they have picked. They also gather chestnuts. In two or three hours, the baskets are full.

That evening everyone has mushrooms for supper. Claudine has cooked them in butter with chopped onion, garlic, and parsley. She has seasoned them with salt and pepper. They smell wonderful and taste delicious. After the mushrooms, Pascal roasts the chestnuts in the fireplace. What a fine end to an October day!

Sometimes when the fall days are sunny, as it was today, Karine and her family eat out in the backyard. Pascal barbecues beef, lamb, or fish, and everything tastes good in the fresh autumn air. Somehow Claudine and Pascal seem less concerned about the children's table manners when they eat outdoors than when they eat indoors. The outdoor meals can get pretty boisterous!

Cooked mushrooms and meat.

The family enjoys a fall supper.

The Festival of St. Romanus

Once a year, in October, everyone celebrates the religious feast of St. Romanus of Rouen, combining it with a local harvest festival. St. Romanus was a bishop who ministered to prisoners over 1,300 years ago. For many years a prisoner was released on his feast day.

Today the celebration is best known for its fair, with a ghost house, a shooting gallery, ring-toss games, show tents, and a merry-go-round. Karine goes every year and likes the merry-go-round and ghost house best. Tanguy is good at ring toss. What he loves best, though, is the ice cream and the big stick of cotton candy his mother buys him.

Whirling along on a carnival ride.

Down the giant slide.

Bumper tag.

Karine meets a classmate, and they go for a spin on the merry-go-round.

Mmmmmm — cotton candy.

Choosing the best slice of meat.

Karine beams when her friends sing and clap for her.

Popcorn, soda, and sweets.

Learning to flip a crêpe into the air.

A butterfly tray with candy.

A Birthday Party

Karine celebrates her birthday by inviting fifteen friends to a party. She has written a play, *Plans for the King,* which she and a few friends perform for the others. The play tells the story of an unfortunate king who has awfully bad luck until at last he marries the woman he loves and bad luck changes to good. Claudine plays background music on the piano. After the play, Karine blows out the candles on her heart-shaped birthday cake, and then everybody dances.

Before the party ends, the children make *crêpes.* People traditionally make these thin, delicate pancakes on Shrove Tuesday (the day before Ash Wednesday). Karine decides to make this tradition part of her birthday celebration. Some people believe that if you can flip the crêpes over, using only one hand to hold the pan, while clutching a coin in your other hand, you will be rich all year. The children try, and find it is not easy.

What is a party without dancing?

Karine dances with one of her favorite friends.

Karine's play, *Plans for the King.*

Karine helps Pascal make a decision.

A Family Christmas

In France, Christmas is called *Nöel*. Preparations to celebrate the birth of Christ begin weeks before December 25. Little children hear how *le père Nöel* (Father Christmas) will bring them presents. Karine and Tanguy both know that père Nöel is not real, but they are excited about Christmas just the same.

Hanging that last ornament on the tree.

On December 24, the Reyssets' house is bustling. Mammi Suzi, Claudine's mother, has come to lend a hand. Everyone pitches in to prepare food, hang decorations, and run errands. Karine and Pascal go off to buy some special cookies at the patisserie and some persimmons, a favorite holiday fruit. By evening, everything is ready.

Placing the Christmas cookies just so on the buffet table.

The Reyssets open gifts on Christmas morning. The stockings they hung from the tree on Christmas Eve are full.

Claudine and Karine go to Christmas Eve Mass. The solemn service lasts almost two hours, with prayers, hymns, and an organ recital. At home, Mammi Suzi, Pascal, and Tanguy set the table for dinner, set out the wine, and make other last-minute preparations.

Soon Claudine and Karine come home. Aunt Jacqueline arrives with her accordion, and everyone eats, chattering excitedly. After dinner they all gather around the glittering Christmas tree to spend the rest of Christmas Eve singing to the accordion — everyone except Tanguy and Pauline, who are tucked in with their Christmas dreams.

An early breakfast! It's still dark outside.

Lots of presents for the children.

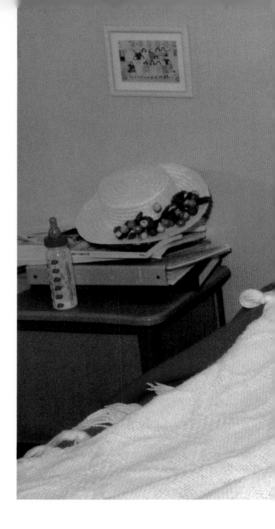

Karine and Tanguy have told their parents what they want for Christmas. Tanguy wants a remote-control car and an Indian tent. Karine is no longer so interested in toys. She would like a sweater, a scarf, and maybe a blouse. Of course, she always wants books.

After a quick breakfast of croissants and hot cocoa, Karine and Tanguy fly to the tree. Hooray! They both got what they were hoping for. Karine and Claudine go to Christmas Day Mass. When they come home, life settles down. The children have another week of winter vacation before they return to school.

Piling into their parents' bed on Christmas morning. Karine and Tanguy are eager to open presents.

The joy of Christmas does not make Karine forget that spring will soon be upon them. The apple trees will once again be in blossom. Karine has had a happy year. She thinks about children in other parts of the world, children who might be her friends if they were to meet. She says, "I think that all the children of the world are members of one big family, for we are not very different from one another and have similar hopes and joys."

FOR YOUR INFORMATION: France

Official Name: République Française
(ray-POO-bleek FRAWN-sehz)
French Republic

Capital: Paris

History

Prehistoric France

People have been living in France for over 30,000 years. Cave paintings at Lascaux, in southern France, date from 17,000 years ago, when Cro-Magnon people lived there. They used tools of stone, bone, and wood. Their descendants became farmers and spread over most of what has become France.

France has been invaded many times. About 900 BC, warlike Celts moved in from central Europe. Invading Romans called them by the Latin word for Celts, *Galli*. From this word, ancient western Europe, including France, became known as Gaul.

The Cathedral of Notre Dame de Paris (Our Lady of Paris).

The Roman Era

In 52 BC, Julius Caesar defeated the last Gallic leader, Vercingetorix, making Gaul a Roman province for over 450 years. The Romans built roads, stone buildings, and aqueducts — structures that resemble bridges but that carry water. Remnants of these structures remain in parts of France. The Romans also established the Roman system of law in Gaul. By the 5th century AD, however, the Roman Empire had collapsed, and Germanic tribes — including the Vandals, the Goths, and the Franks — began invading Gaul. In AD 486, Clovis, a Frankish chieftain who had adopted Christianity, conquered the last of Roman Gaul and became the first Frankish king. The name *France* comes from the Latin word *Francia*, which means "land of the Franks."

Feudalism, the Vikings, and a United Nobility

During the Middle Ages, the period stretching from AD 476 to 1453, people lived in a feudal system; serfs worked the fields for the owners of large estates, called manors. The serfs gave much of their produce to these owners in exchange for protection from quarrels going on between rival tribes. In time, these tribes began to unite. By 732, Franks began invading neighboring nations. When Charlemagne became emperor of the Holy Roman Empire, in 800, the empire included France, Germany, northern Italy, and northeastern Spain, as well as large areas of land stretching well into eastern Europe.

Under Charlemagne (Charles the Great), the empire prospered, although his rule could be harsh: many people were forced to become Christians at swordpoint. When he died in 814, his sons divided the land, and the power of the empire began to weaken. At about this time, seafaring Vikings began to attack.

In 911, Charles III conceded the area around Rouen to these Vikings, called Norsemen, "northmen." They represented three areas — Norway, Sweden, and Denmark; those invading France were probably Danish. The area they settled they called Normandy, after Norseman (Norman) conquerers. Not until 1450 would France again control this area, which passed from Norman to English rulers.

In 1066, the Normans, under William the Conqueror, sailed north and conquered England. For many years, they held sway over both England and large portions of land in France. When Matilda, daughter of King Henry I of England, married Frenchman Geoffrey of Anjou, English and French families united, making it possible for the English and French to control land in both countries. When their son became king of England in 1154, he exercised power in France as well as in England.

By 1204, King Philip Augustus of France had won back portions of Normandy and other English lands in France. From 1337 to 1453, England and France battled in a conflict called the Hundred Years' War, during the time when the terrible plague, the Black Death, killed about one-third of its people. The weakened French, encouraged by 19-year-old Joan of Arc, resisted the English. Joan claimed she was inspired by heavenly "voices." She was captured and, in 1431, was burned at the stake as a heretic, one who publicly questions church beliefs. France won the war, and Joan of Arc was later proclaimed a saint.

Religious Intolerance and Lavish Living

France had been Roman Catholic since Clovis ruled in 486. Then, in the 16th century, some people began protesting for reforms in the Roman Catholic Church. In France, these Protestants, called Huguenots, battled with Catholics for control of the nation. Finally, in 1598, a new king, Henry of Navarre, originally a Huguenot, proclaimed in the Edict of Nantes that Protestants could practice their faith; to satisfy Catholics, he had converted to Catholicism. Almost 100 years later, the proclamation was revoked, so Huguenots fled to England, Germany, Switzerland, the Netherlands, and North America, places that allowed them to practice their faith freely.

King Louis XIII, Henry's son, was not so tactful a ruler, so during his reign, from 1610 to 1643, his advisers, Cardinals Armand Jean du Plessis Richelieu and Jules Mazarin, had to further Henry's goals of improving commerce, keeping peace, and reducing the power of the nobility. Louis XIV, the "Sun King," who ruled from 1643 to 1715, increased the king's power. In his gorgeous palace at Versailles, he held elaborate balls and entertainments — while his soldiers went off to conquer other lands. It was mostly the middle class and the peasants who paid for these wars. It was Louis XIV who revoked the Edict of Nantes.

Louis XV also loved pleasure, but unlike Louis XIV, he allowed the power of the throne to weaken. His successor, Louis XVI, with his Austrian wife, Marie Antoinette, continued the lavish style of this family. When he failed to solve the increasing problems facing France's divided people, the stage was set for radical change.

Revolution and Napoleon Bonaparte

The people resented a king who had all the power; they resented subsidizing wars and lavish entertainment. They were reading about the rights of citizens in the works of Jean Jacques Rousseau and other French writers. They knew about and in fact were helping to support the American Revolution. In 1789 an assembly met to demand reforms; a mob of citizens attacked the Bastille, a royal prison in Paris. The French Revolution had begun. King Louis XVI was deposed in 1792. The next year, he and Marie Antoinette were beheaded. In a period called the Reign of Terror, many innocent people who supported the monarchy or who merely disagreed with the new government were put to death by guillotine. But after the revolution and the Reign of Terror, the French people began to build a new society.

The French also defended their revolution against other supporters of the monarchy. The great French militarist, Napoleon Bonaparte, became the leader of France and in 1804 crowned himself emperor. In the years that followed, he conquered much of Europe. But one winter, when invading Russia, he weakened. By 1814, he gave up his power and was exiled to the island of Elba, in the Mediterranean Sea. But there, he amassed an army and returned to France to fight his conquerors, only to be defeated on June 18, 1815, at the Battle of Waterloo. He was exiled to St. Helena, an island in the Atlantic, where he died in 1821.

More Revolution

After Napoleon's rule, the monarchy returned, wanting the power kings had had before the revolution. When, after the July Revolution of 1830, one king resigned and another, Louis Philippe, became the first French monarch to rule with the permission of the people and under the limits of a written constitution.

But in 1848 France had another revolution, Louis Philippe was deposed, and the Second Republic was declared. Louis Napoleon, a nephew of Napoleon Bonaparte, became emperor in 1852. He ruled until 1870 when Prussia, now part of Germany, invaded France and forced him to surrender. The Third Republic was established. France ceded Alsace and part of Lorraine to Germany.

La Belle Époque and World Wars I and II

But from 1871 to 1914 France enjoyed a peaceful time called in French la Belle Époque, the beautiful era. During this period, the arts flourished and life was pleasant for the French. But then, in 1914, World War I began. Germany invaded France, which became a battleground for four years. In 1918, the Allies — including France, Great Britain, the United States, and Canada — defeated Germany. Alsace and Lorraine, taken by the Germans, were returned to France under the Treaty of Versailles. France had lost almost 1.4 million men in the war and was further weakened by the Great Depression, which destroyed businesses and individuals throughout the West. In the 1930s, it began worrying about the military buildup under Adolf Hitler in Germany. But many people thought they were safe from German attack because of the Maginot Line of guns, tank barriers, and other defenses along the border between France and Germany.

In 1939 World War II began. In 1940, Germany went around the Maginot Line, France surrendered, and the nation lived under Nazi rule until 1944, when Allied troops liberated the nation. During the war, parts of France not occupied by Nazi troops were governed by a Frenchman, Marshal Henri Philippe Pétain, a hero in World War I. Unfortunately, in ruling what was called Vichy France, he was often like the Nazis he cooperated with.

People joined the underground French Resistance movement to oppose the Germans. In England, Charles de Gaulle headed the Free French forces and temporarily headed the government after 1944.

After the war, the French established the Fourth Republic and joined the North Atlantic Treaty Organization (NATO) for the defense of Europe and the European Economic Community (EEC) to break down trade barriers in Europe. France lost some colonies, including Vietnam, and encountered serious unrest in Algeria.

Charles de Gaulle, president of the Fifth Republic from 1958 to 1969, granted independence to Algeria but withdrew French forces from NATO. From 1969 to 1981, two relatively moderate presidents, Georges Pompidou and Valery Giscard d'Estaing, led France. Then, in 1981, François Mitterrand, a Socialist, was elected. His prime minister is Michel Rocard. The 1960s through the 1980s have brought great change to France. Before World War II, France was primarily agricultural, with Paris as the great center of culture, commerce, and government. Now, like many Western countries, it has become an important industrial and economic force in the world. The nation has seen growth in the cultural life of cities beyond Paris.

Population and Ethnic Groups

In 1986 the population of France was over 55 million. About 80% of the people live in cities or towns; the rest live in small villages or on farms. France's people come from various ethnic groups. Near the Mediterranean, many people have the dark eyes and olive skin typical of Latin people. In northwestern France, some people have light hair and skin and blue eyes, like their Norse ancestors. The French who descended from the ancient Celts of central and western Europe tend to be shorter and darker. Many people in Alsace and Lorraine resemble the Germans who intermarried and settled there during their rule. In recent years, new immigrants have added African and Oriental elements to the population. Like North America, France is a melting pot, and many people show a mixture of ethnic features.

Government

The current government, called the Fifth Republic, is based upon the 1958 constitution. The French vote at age 18. Their president, who serves seven years, appoints a prime minister and a council of ministers as advisers. He is head of the armed forces, makes treaties, and helps the parliament set policy. The parliament consists of a National Assembly and a Senate. The 577 Assembly members serve for five years, while the 319 Senate members serve for nine. The Assembly has more power. It can pass laws and vote the president and his assistants out of office. But the president can dissolve the Assembly and call for a new election.

France has two court systems. One, the Council of State, handles problems between governmental offices and citizens. The other, the Court of Cassation, takes care of matters such as basic civil and criminal cases.

The smallest unit of government is the commune — cities, towns, and villages. Each commune elects a council and a mayor, and each belongs to a metropolitan department. There are 96 of these departments; they are somewhat like counties in the US. The 96 departments form 22 larger administrative regions.

Language

Like Spanish, Italian, and Portuguese, French developed from Latin, spoken by the Romans, and is therefore called a Romance language, from Roman. French was once the international language, spoken by those who carried on world affairs of business, education, religion, and government. Today English is more widely used, but French remains important. People speak it in parts of Belgium and Switzerland, as well as in former French colonies like Quebec, Haiti, and parts of Africa and Asia.

French dialects differ, as do dialects of any language. People from Paris consider their pronunciation of words to be the best. In some parts of France, people also speak other languages. In Brittany, it is Breton; in the western Pyrenees, it is Basque; in the eastern Pyrenees, it is Catalan; in Alsace and Lorraine, it is a German dialect; in parts of the Alps and on Corsica are dialects close to Italian.

The French want to keep their language unchanged; they want no words stealing in from other languages. An institution called the *Académie Française,* the French Academy, tries to prevent foreign words from entering the French language. But in French cities, you can see or hear expressions like "le hot dog" or "le drug store."

Religion

Over 80% of the French people are Roman Catholic, but less than half go to church regularly. About 3% of the people are Muslim, 2% are Protestant, and 1% are Jewish, the largest population of Jews in western Europe.

Christianity spread through France from the second century AD onward, and much art and architecture have arisen around the Roman Catholic

The Louvre in Paris, a world-famous art museum.

faith. During the 8th century, a chapel to Saint Michel (the archangel Michael) was built high on a rock near the sea and named Mont-Saint-Michel (Saint Michael Mountain). During high tide, no one could reach the chapel. In the 11th century, monks began erecting a huge monastery here; visitors had to brave the tides or the mud. From the 10th through 11th centuries, other religious orders became wealthy and built massive structures in France. By the 13th century, the middle class helped pay for such Gothic cathedrals as Saint-Denis, Notre Dame, Amiens, Chartres, Rouen, Reims, and Sainte-Chapelle. Most of these magnificent structures are open to visitors who wish to study the architecture of centuries ago. Now, a permanent road enables them to reach Mont-Saint-Michel even during high tide.

The Arts

Over the centuries, the French have produced great writers. Like the literature of many other peoples, early French literature was a form of oral poetry, poems that were chanted or sung. These poems, called *chansons de geste* ("songs of heroic exploit") detail the deeds of great heroes — Christian heroes, because France has long been predominantly Roman Catholic. The oral poets, called *jongleurs* in French, composed their songs as they traveled the countryside, joining with caravans of travelers and staying in the halls of wealthy people. They recited at gatherings, keeping the rhythm by strumming on a stringed instrument. In time, as writing developed, some of this oral literature was preserved through writing.

Early writers used Latin, the written language of scholars. But by the 11th century, they had begun to use French. By the 13th century, poets wrote about other subjects besides Christian heroes. In the fable, they made fun of the upper classes, and slyly masked criticism of these classes by using animals as characters. In the lyric poem, they wrote about love and other abstract ideas such as truth and fidelity.

It was not until the 16th century that literature began to be written in prose as well as poetry. Today, one children's book in prose is perhaps as popular with adults as with children. It is Antoine de Saint-Exupéry's *The Little Prince*. This gentle fable includes a talking fox, a boa constrictor that has swallowed an elephant, a tiny prince, and a stranded airline pilot — among other intriguing characters. *The Little Prince* is so popular that it has been translated into many languages and can be found in libraries across North America.

Currency

The official currency is the *franc*. One franc equals 100 *centimes*. As of 1988, one US dollar was worth about six francs.

Land

France — including its island, Corsica — is the largest country in western Europe, at about 210,000 square miles (544,000 sq km), about four-fifths the size of Texas and somewhat smaller than Manitoba. At its widest points, it measures about 600 miles (960 km) both north to south and east to west.

It is bordered on the northwest by the English Channel and the Strait of Dover, in the North Sea, and on the west by the Atlantic. Part of its southern boundary is the Pyrenees Mountains, separating France from Spain, and part is formed by the Mediterranean Sea. On the east, the Alps separate France from Switzerland and Italy, and the Rhine River forms part of the border between France and West Germany. The northeast border runs beside Germany and Belgium to the Strait of Dover. So close to major waterways, France has been a power on the sea. It stands between the Atlantic and most of the rest of western Europe, so it has also been able to influence its neighbors.

France has lowlands, hills, mountains, and seacoasts. Most of the land is less than 850 feet (260 m) above sea level. But Mont Blanc, at 15,770 feet (4,800 m) is the tallest mountain in western Europe. Major mountain ranges — the Pyrenees, Alps, Jura, and Vosges — are near the edges of France. The Massif Central, an area of high and rocky plateaus and mountains covering about one-sixth of France's land, is in south central France. It separates the subtropical part of Mediterranean France from the cooler northern sections.

Many towns and cities have grown up along the rivers. Paris, in the midst of the large and fertile Paris Basin, spreads out on both banks of the Seine River, which flows into the Atlantic near Le Havre. Strasbourg is on the Rhine, which is one of Europe's main waterways. The Rhône River begins in the Alps and flows past Lyon and Avignon to the Mediterranean. A number of dams generate electricity on the Rhône. The Saône and Rhône rivers follow a great lowland furrow west of the Alps. The Loire is the longest river that is completely in France. Because it often overflows its banks, it is lined by many levees. Along its length grow many vineyards. There are many other, smaller, rivers and a number of canals. All of these waterways have made water an important means of transportation in France.

Climate

France's climate varies a lot for a small country. Winds from Africa keep the south mild in the winter and hot in the summer, because the Mediterranean is too small and warm to cool the breezes much as they blow north to France. The currents of the Atlantic give western France, especially Britanny and Normandy, cool, rainy summers and mild winters. Farther from the ocean, northern France has mild summers and cold winters. Rain and snow occur in the mountains; even in summer the evenings are very cool.

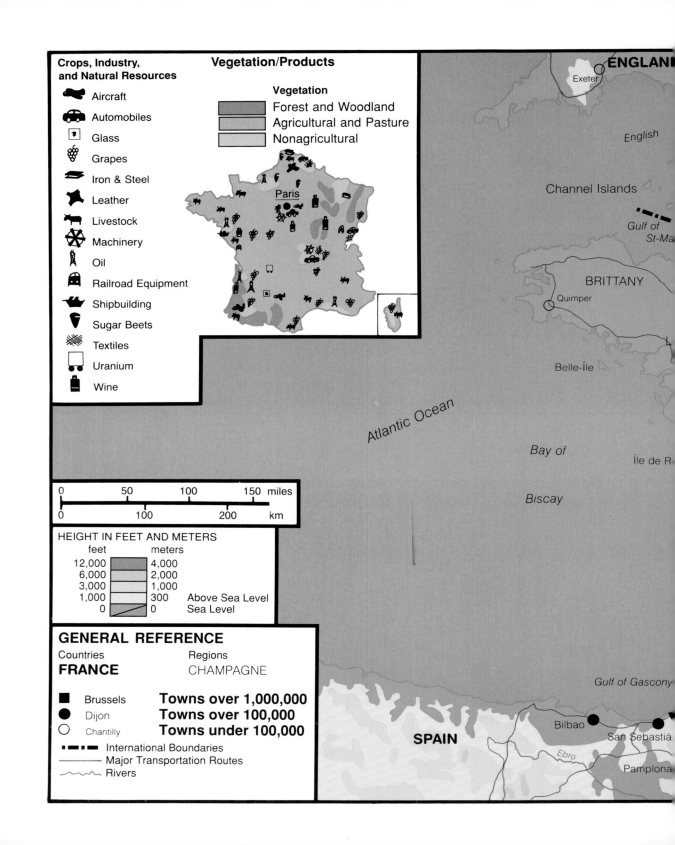

Crops, Industry, and Natural Resources

- Aircraft
- Automobiles
- Glass
- Grapes
- Iron & Steel
- Leather
- Livestock
- Machinery
- Oil
- Railroad Equipment
- Shipbuilding
- Sugar Beets
- Textiles
- Uranium
- Wine

Vegetation/Products

Vegetation

- Forest and Woodland
- Agricultural and Pasture
- Nonagricultural

Paris

0	50	100	150 miles
0	100	200	km

HEIGHT IN FEET AND METERS

feet	meters	
12,000	4,000	
6,000	2,000	
3,000	1,000	
1,000	300	Above Sea Level
0	0	Sea Level

GENERAL REFERENCE

Countries   Regions
FRANCE   CHAMPAGNE

- ■ Brussels   **Towns over 1,000,000**
- ● Dijon   **Towns over 100,000**
- ○ Chantilly   **Towns under 100,000**
- ▄▀▄▀ International Boundaries
- —— Major Transportation Routes
- 〜〜 Rivers

ENGLAND

Exeter

English

Channel Islands

Gulf of St-Ma

BRITTANY

Quimper

Belle-Île

Atlantic Ocean

Bay of

Biscay

Île de R

Gulf of Gascony

Bilbao

San Sebastiá

SPAIN

Ebro

Pamplona

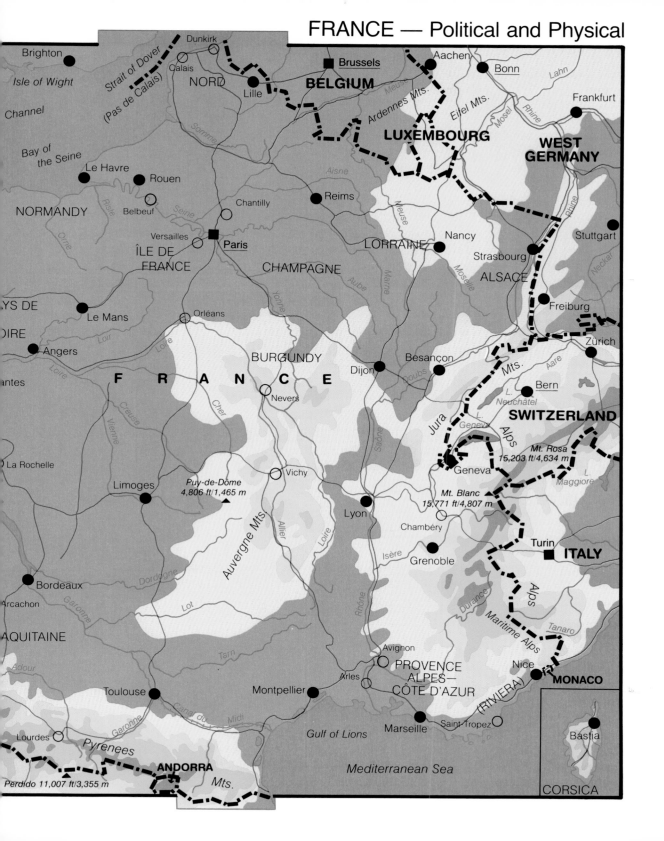

FRANCE — Political and Physical

Brighton

Isle of Wight

Channel

Strait of Dover
(Pas de Calais)

Dunkirk

Calais

NORD

Lille

Brussels

BELGIUM

Aachen

Bonn

Frankfurt

Ardennes Mts.

Eifel Mts.

Meuse

Mosel

Rhine

Lahn

LUXEMBOURG

WEST
GERMANY

Bay of
the Seine

Le Havre

Rouen

Belbeuf

NORMANDY

Riste

Orne

Seine

Somme

Aisne

Chantilly

Reims

Meuse

Nancy

Moselle

Strasbourg

Stuttgart

Neckar

ALSACE

Versailles

Paris

ÎLE DE
FRANCE

CHAMPAGNE

Aube

Marne

LORRAINE

Freiburg

LYS DE
OIRE

Le Mans

Angers

antes

La Rochelle

F   R   A   N   C   E

Orléans

Loir

Loire

Cher

Creuse

Vienne

BURGUNDY

Nevers

Yonne

Dijon

Besançon

Doubs

Saône

Mts.

Jura

Zürich

Aare

Bern

L.
Neuchâtel

SWITZERLAND

L.
Geneva

Alps

Mt. Rosa
15,203 ft/4,634 m

Geneva

L.
Maggiore

Limoges

Puy-de-Dôme
4,806 ft/1,465 m

Vichy

Auvergne Mts.

Allier

Loire

Lyon

Mt. Blanc
15,771 ft/4,807 m

Chambéry

Isère

Grenoble

Turin

ITALY

Alps

Bordeaux

Arcachon

Garonne

Dordogne

Lot

AQUITAINE

Tarn

Durance

Maritime Alps

Tanaro

Toulouse

Montpellier

Avignon

Arles

PROVENCE
ALPES—
CÔTE D'AZUR

Nice

MONACO

(RIVIERA)

Lourdes

Pyrenees

Canal du Midi

Garonne

Adour

ANDORRA

Perdido 11,007 ft/3,355 m

Mts.

Gulf of Lions

Marseille

Saint-Tropez

Mediterranean Sea

Bastia

CORSICA

Natural Resources

Centuries ago France was almost totally covered with forests. Today only about a quarter of the land is wooded. The government encourages conserving trees and reforesting the land. Today, wood is seldom used as a fuel or for house construction but instead appears in boxes, flooring, furniture, resins, and turpentine. Wood does provide some pulp for paper, but France also has to import wood pulp and paper to meet its needs.

France is not rich in minerals. But the iron deposits in Lorraine are the largest in western Europe, and Normandy and the Massif Central have some iron ore deposits. There are deposits of copper, zinc, lead, potash (used in fertilizers), and bauxite, the ore from which aluminum is produced. Some coal deposits remain in France, but mining costs are high because the deposits are so deep. In western Europe, France is behind only West Germany and Italy in steel production.

Deposits of natural gas, mostly in the Pyrenees, have supplied up to two-thirds of the gas used in France, but the nation is exhausting these deposits. While some oil comes from French-owned Algerian oil fields, France must also import oil from the Middle East. France is the world's seventh largest producer of uranium, used in nuclear plants to generate electricity.

The fast-moving waters of the many rivers also provide electric power. Near St-Malo, in Brittany, a large power plant is capturing the power of the ocean tides. The ocean also provides fish and seafood: cod, mackerel, sardines, and herring and, in the Bay of Biscay in the Atlantic, oysters.

Industry

The French have long been known for the design and crafting of their products. Since World War II, they have been focusing on heavy industry and mass production. If we measure France's position according to the total value of its goods and services, the nation is fifth among the industrial nations — after the United States, the Soviet Union, Japan, and West Germany.

The industries in northern France produce coal, iron and steel, heavy machinery, engineering tools, and locomotives. In Paris, small factories and workshops produce clothing, jewelry, toys, luxury items, and chemicals such as dyes, perfumes, and pharmaceuticals. On the outskirts of Paris are plants that manufacture cars, aircraft, food products, machine tools, and electrical and engineering equipment.

In the south, companies produce tires, railroad equipment, armaments, textiles, china, and engineering products. In Marseilles there are petroleum-refining and petrochemical plants. France also produces rockets used to send satellites into space for the European space program.

Agriculture

Because of its generally mild climate, adequate rain, and fertile soil, France leads western Europe agriculturally. Large areas of flat land make it easy to farm with machinery. At one time, when parents died, farms were divided into small, often scattered, parcels for children. Government policies prevent that now, and the government helps farmers put together larger tracts of land so they can farm more efficiently. Although some still use tools like wooden pitchforks on small farms in the hilly areas, most farmers use modern machinery and methods. After World War II, 36% of the people lived on farms; today only 8% farm, yet they produce more.

The most valuable crop is wheat — France is fifth in the world. It also produces many tons of sugar beets as well as hay and turnips, which are raised to feed animals. The many varieties of grapes that grow have made France second only to Italy in wine production. The French also grow potatoes, corn, barley, vegetables, and fruit as well as flowers to sell and to use in making perfume.

Much of the land in Normandy and Brittany is in pasture, which provides grazing land for cattle. The dairy industry has become famous for its cheeses. Hogs, cattle, and poultry are also important as a meat source; they bring in about 60% of the country's farm income. In fact, France is western Europe's leading food exporter.

Education

France has a long history of high culture and education for those who could afford it. Today the government sees that all are educated up to age 16. Ninety-eight percent of the French can read and write.

Most French children, some as young as two years old, attend nursery school or kindergarten. All children go to school from the ages of six to sixteen. Most attend public schools, but about one-fifth attend Catholic and other private schools.

The first four years of secondary school are called *collège*; the last three are called *lycée*. Instead of attending academic lycées, some students go on to technical schools to learn carpentry, electrical work, or other skilled trades. Others prepare for the *baccalauréat* examination to enter a university. Some do additional work so they can attend *grandes écoles*, institutions that train people for high-level careers in government, education, industry, or the military.

Although the formality of French education has relaxed recently, strict discipline and respect for teachers remain. Even younger students have at least two hours of homework every night. Students attend school from 9 a.m. to 4:30 p.m. On Wednesdays, many schools are closed, and children have sports and clubs, which are separate from school. Many students then go to school on Saturday mornings.

Sports

The most popular spectator sporting event is the Tour de France bicycle marathon. In summer, professional bicyclists race cross-country while fans follow their progress. Soccer is a favorite team sport, with many spectators. French employers give workers at least five weeks of vacation a year, so the French have become active in sports. Skiing, boating, tennis, and hiking are popular. Men gather to play *pétanque*, or *boules*, a kind of outdoor bowling game in which players roll metal balls at a small wooden ball.

France's famous high-speed train, the TGV, can go 170 miles (274 km) an hour.

Paris

Paris, the hub of France, is crowded with native Parisians, immigrants, refugees, and visitors from around the world. A center of culture, commerce, and fashion for France and the West, Paris is rich with museums, libraries, art galleries, and theaters. Notre Dame and other world-famous buildings and monuments are flooded with light at night for all to see. Maybe that is why Paris is called the "City of Light." It is also the capital of France.

From the top of the Eiffel Tower, you would not see a skyline of skyscrapers. You might spy some tall buildings, but mostly you would see blue-gray slate roofs of centuries-old apartment houses and shops, domes of public buildings, and spires of cathedrals. You would see the Seine River, with old, elegant bridges joining its riverbanks and people strolling along its banks or sitting at outdoor tables in cafés.

French in North America

The French have played a major role in the history of North America. Look for the names mentioned below on buildings, street signs, and maps. Between 1534 and 1542, Frenchman Jacques Cartier and his crews made three voyages up the St. Lawrence River to the sites of present-day Montreal and Quebec City. From then on, French fishermen, hunters, and trappers traveled through the forests of North America. In the 17th century, French explorer Samuel de Champlain mapped the Atlantic Coast from Nova Scotia to Martha's Vineyard. Other Frenchmen explored the Great Lakes in canoes. In 1673, Jesuit missionaries Jacques Marquette and Louis Joliet followed the lakes, rivers, and portages to the Mississippi River. Nine years later, René Robert Cavalier, sieur de La Salle, became the first European to travel to the mouth of the Mississippi; he claimed all land whose rivers drained to the Mississippi for Louis XIV.

By the early 18th century, "New France" extended from the mouth of the Mississippi north into Canada. Some of the French had settled in northeastern Canada, in an area called Acadia. Along the Mississippi and at Pittsburgh, the French built forts and established a fur-trading center at Detroit.

But the British also held parts of North America, and conflicts between the nations developed because of religious differences. The British forced out French Acadians, who settled in Louisiana, where they became known as "Cajuns" (from the original "Acadians"). Their descendants, famous for their music and cooking, still live in Louisiana and Texas. Other French immigrants helped settle New Orleans, today the most French of US cities. Their descendants, known as Creoles, are an elegant cultural mix of black, French, and Spanish elements.

More French came in 1849-50, during the California Gold Rush, although most did not settle permanently. Others came at times of unrest in France — the Huguenots during the religious wars, the aristocracy during the French Revolution, and supporters of Napoleon Bonaparte after he was deposed. Many emigrants settled in New England mill towns and worked in the textile mills, living in poor housing in segregated French neighborhoods.

About seven million people of French descent live in Canada, mostly in Quebec. In the 1960s and 1970s, some wanted Quebec to separate from Canada and become a French-speaking nation. Today Canada has remained unified and, particularly in Quebec, Canadians use both the French and English languages. In the US, about 14 million people, at least in part, are descended from the French. They live all over the United States, except for concentrations in Louisiana and New England, and work in all sorts of trades and professions.

Glossary of Useful French Terms

baguette (bah-GET) .... a long, narrow loaf of bread
boulangerie (boo-LAHN-zjer-ee) .... bakery
café au lait (ka-FAY oh lay) .... coffee with milk, a popular drink for adults
château (shah-TOE) .... a large country house
crêpe (krep) .... a thin, light pancake
école (AY-kole) .... school
mère (mare) .... mother
père (pare) .... father

More Books About France

Look for these books at your local library or bookstore, or ask someone there to order them for you. They will help you do research for the "Things to Do" section.

France. Editors of Time-Life Books (Time-Life Books)
France. Lifschitz (Silver Burdett)
France: The Crossroads of Europe. Balerdi (Dillon)
Here Is France. Bishop (Farrar, Straus & Giroux)

Things to Do — Research Projects

Since France gave up its control of Vietnam and Algeria, it has concentrated its attention on domestic policies, decisions concerning the daily lives of its citizens. As you read about events in France, keep in mind the importance of current facts. Some of the projects that follow need accurate information, so try to use up-to-date newspapers and magazines. Two library publications will help you find recent articles on many topics, so just look up the word *France* in them.

Readers' Guide to Periodical Literature
Children's Magazine Guide

1. Think of an occupation or career that interests you. In France, do both men and women enter this field? Is schooling available for this work? Once out of school, would you be able to find a position in this occupation?

2. What are the leading industries in France? What do they make? Who do they trade with? Do they export their goods to North America?

More Things to Do — Activities

These projects should encourage you to think more about France. They offer ideas for interesting group or individual projects you can do at school or at home.

1. Invite someone from France to visit your class and tell you about France. Or, if no French people live in your area, invite the teacher of French class from your school, or perhaps a student who knows French and the French culture quite well.

2. If you were going to talk to a child from France, what questions would you ask?

3. If you would like a pen pal in France, write to these people:

International Pen Friends
P.O. Box 290065
Brooklyn, NY 11229

Worldwide Pen Friends
P.O. Box 6896
Thousand Oaks, CA 91359

Tell them you want a pen pal from France and include your name and address.

Index